GET READ...

FOR ONE-OCTAVE SCALE DUETS!

by Wynn-Anne Rossi and Lucy Wilde Warren

SCALE DUETS

Check Off (✓) when completed successfully with duet

INSTRUCTIONAL ACTIVITY PAGES

Soft Shoe in C

W. Rossi

Both hands two octaves higher

NOTE: After all the *major scales* have been mastered, it is suggested that the student cycle back through the book to play them again, along with their relative minors.

Teacher duet

Relaxed, with a swing

Soft Shoe in A Minor

W. Rossi

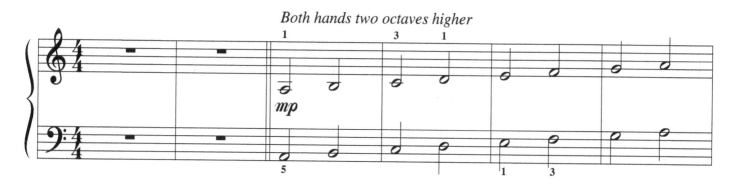

Teacher duet

Jitterbug in G

W. Rossi

Both hands one octave higher

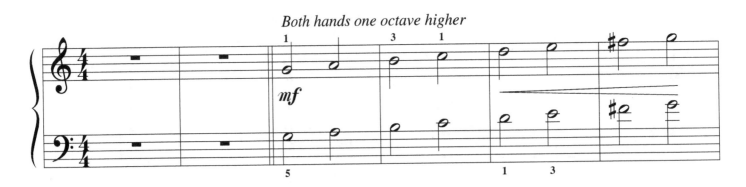

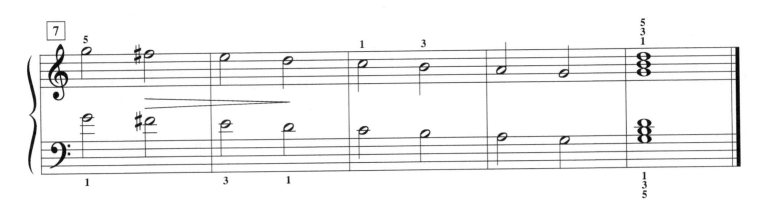

Teacher duet
Lively, with a swing

Jitterbug in E Minor

W. Rossi

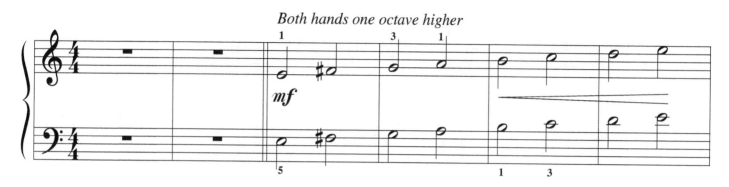

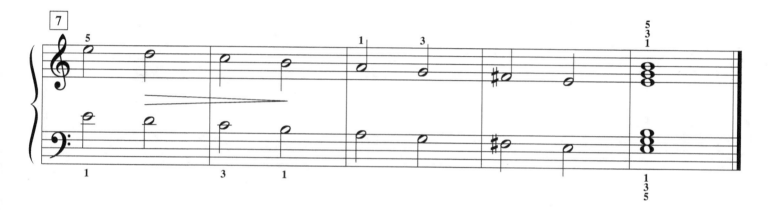

Teacher duet

Cool, with a swing

New York Taxi in D

W. Rossi

Both hands two octaves higher

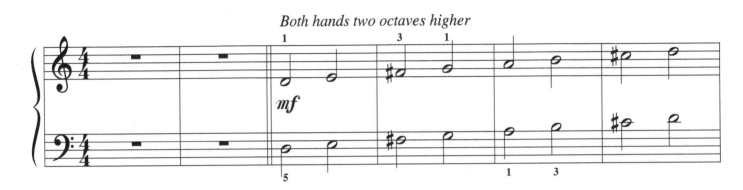

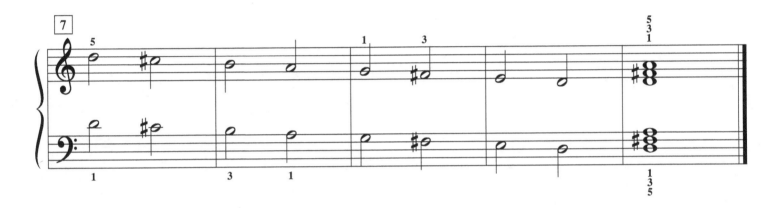

Teacher duet

Cheerful and busy

New York Taxi in B Minor

W. Rossi

Both hands two octaves higher

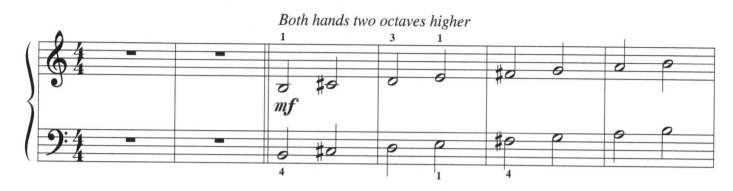

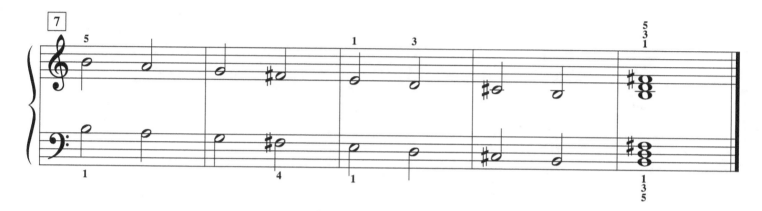

Teacher duet

A little grumpy

FJH1679

Rock Out in A

W. Rossi

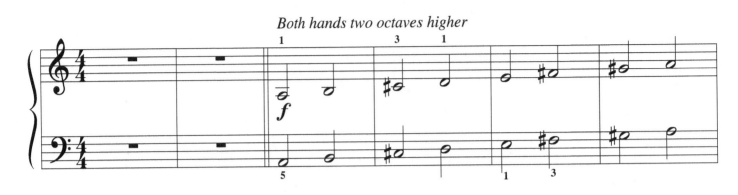

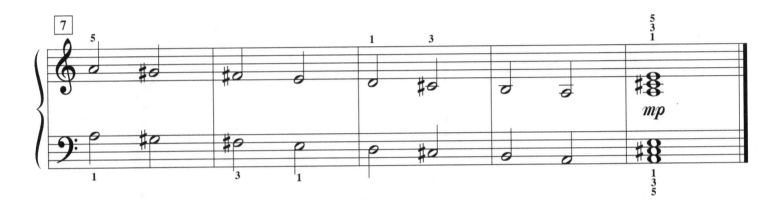

Teacher duet

Rock Out in F♯ Minor

W. Rossi

Lazy Blues in E

W. Rossi

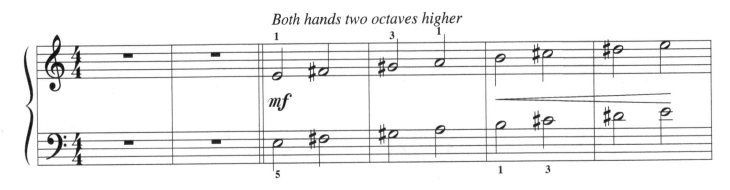

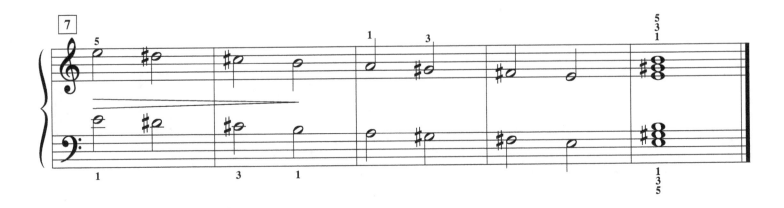

Teacher duet

Lazy Blues in C♯ Minor

W. Rossi

Both hands two octaves higher

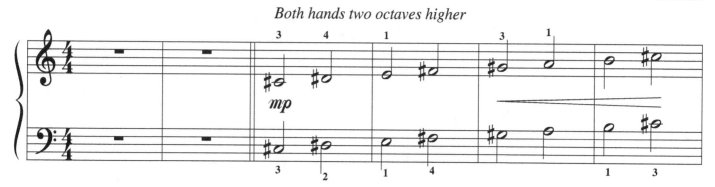

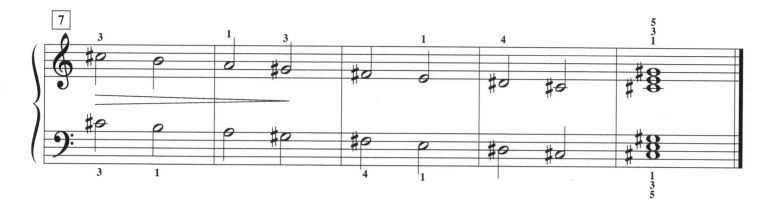

Teacher duet

Lazy, with a swing

Boogie-Woogie in B

W. Rossi

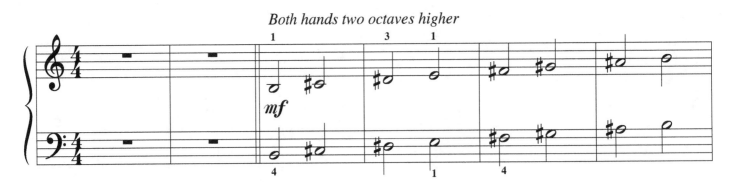

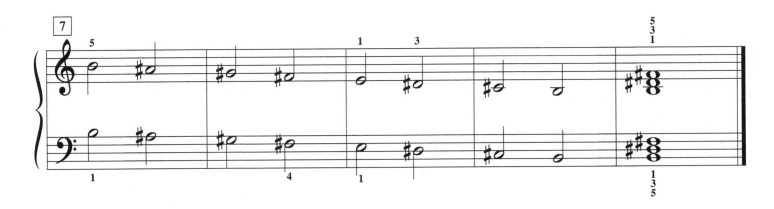

Teacher duet

Boogie-Woogie in G♯ Minor

W. Rossi

Both hands one octave higher

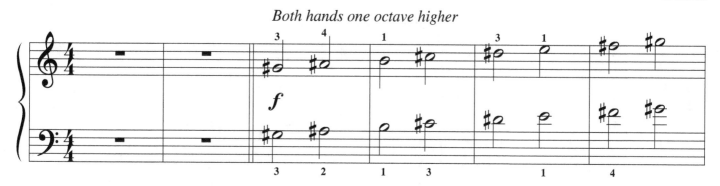

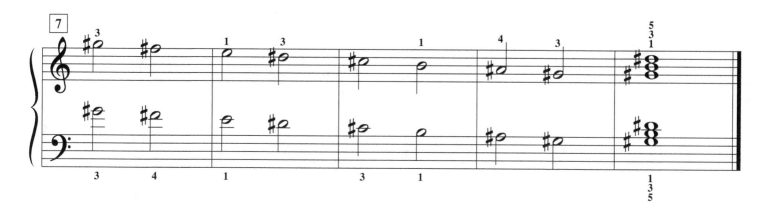

Teacher duet

Cruisin' in F

L.W. Warren

Both hands two octaves higher

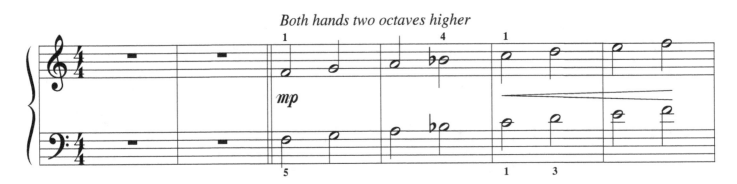

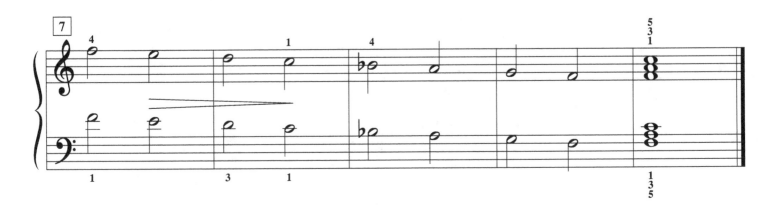

Teacher duet

Cruisin' in D Minor

L.W. Warren

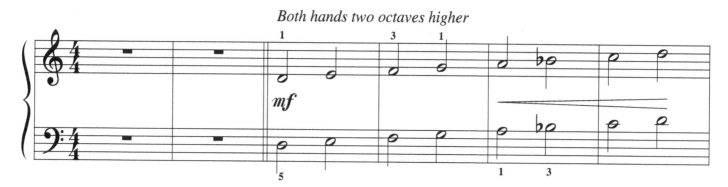

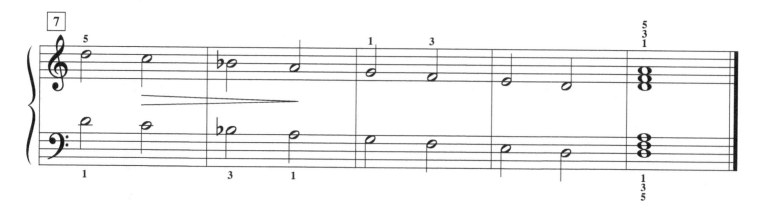

Teacher duet

Brassy Beat in B♭

W. Rossi

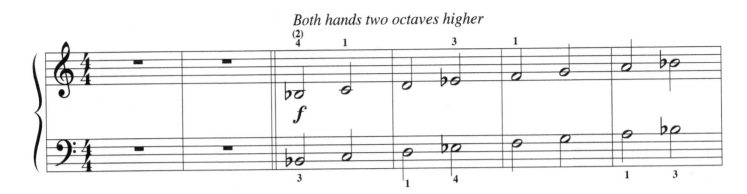

Teacher duet

Brassy Beat in G Minor

W. Rossi

Both hands one octave higher

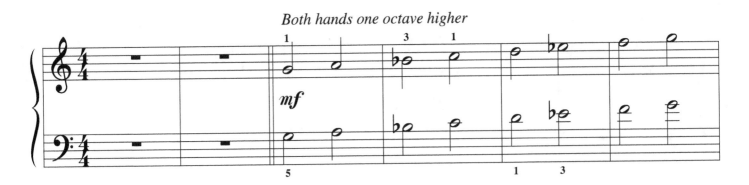

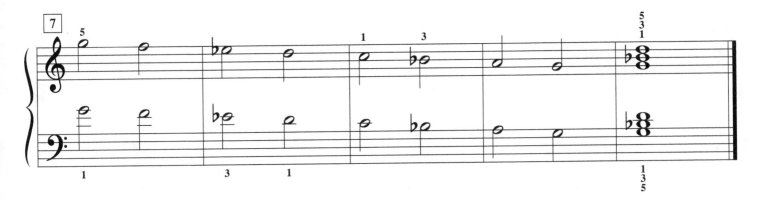

Teacher duet

Swing it!

L.H. detached

Heart or Soul in E♭

W. Rossi

Both hands two octaves higher

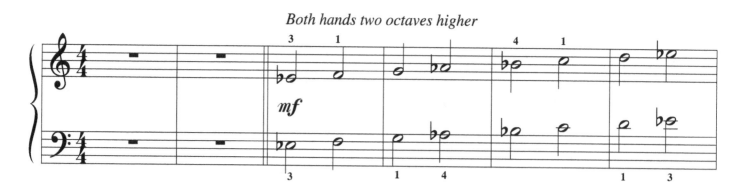

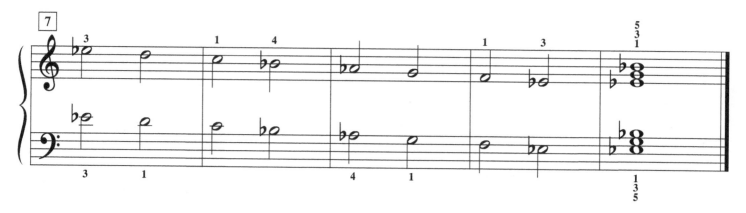

Teacher duet

With a happy swing

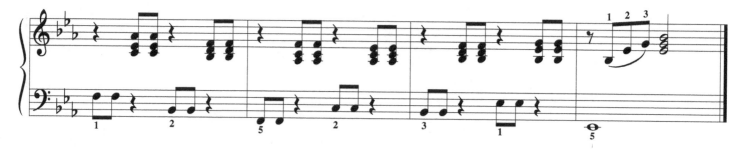

Heart or Soul in C Minor

W. Rossi

Both hands two octaves higher

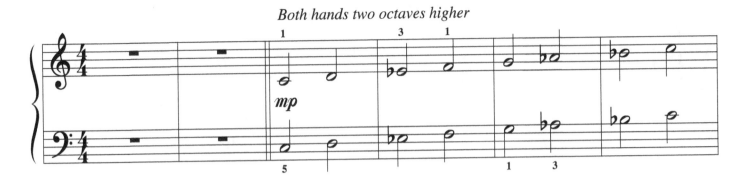

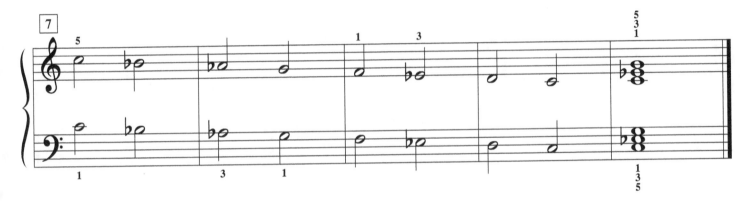

Teacher duet

With a gentle swing

Latin Sounds in A♭

W. Rossi

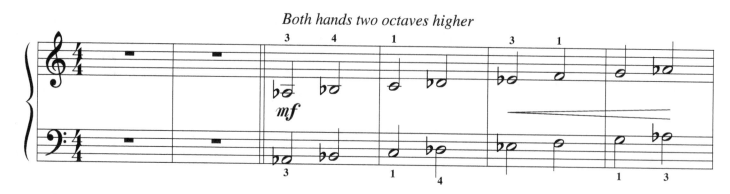

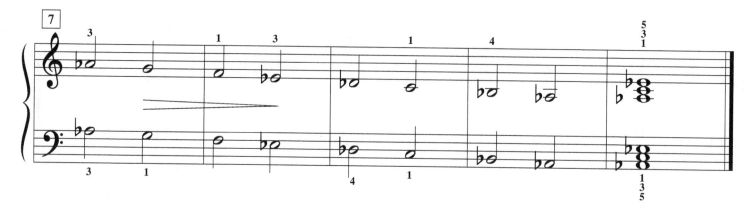

Teacher duet

Latin Sounds in F Minor

W. Rossi

Both hands one octave higher

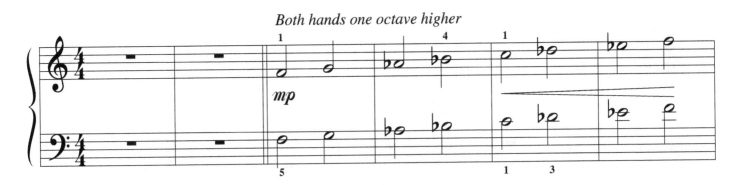

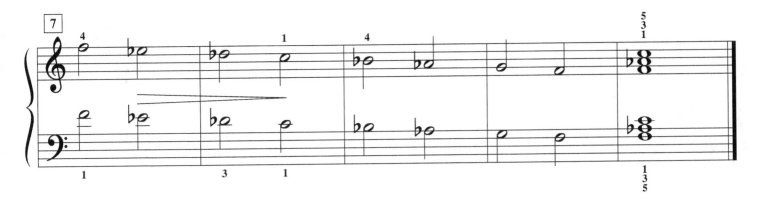

Teacher duet

Smoothly

Miami Moon in D♭

L.W. Warren

Both hands two octaves higher

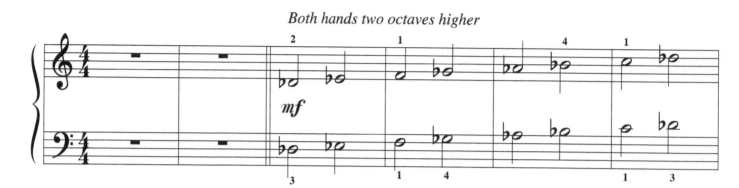

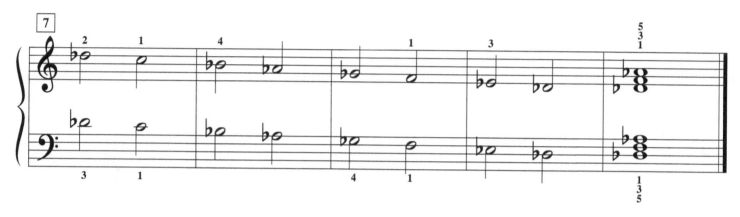

Teacher duet

Miami Moon in B♭ Minor

L.W. Warren

Both hands two octaves higher

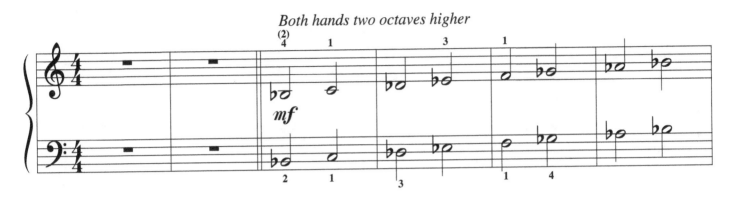

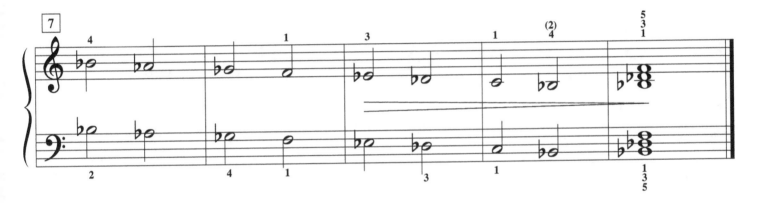

Teacher duet

Leisurely

Chillin' in G♭

W. Rossi

Both hands two octaves higher

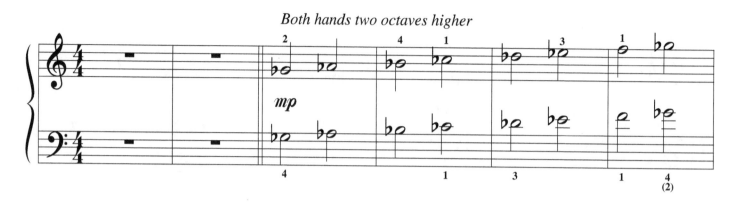

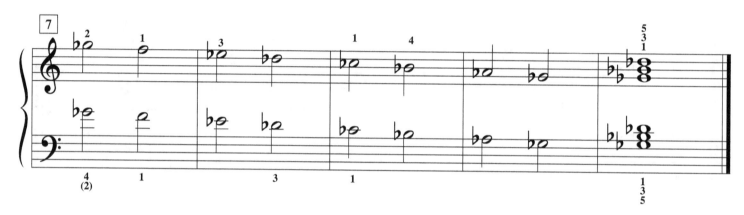

Teacher duet

With a cool swing

Chillin' in E♭ Minor

W. Rossi

Both hands two octaves higher

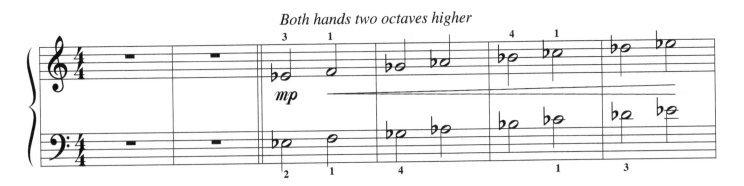

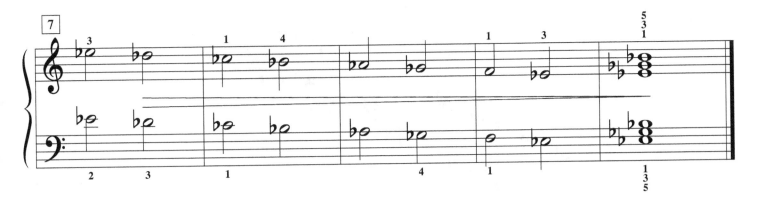

Teacher duet

Stepping Up to Major and Minor Scales

Major Scales

> A one-octave major scale is made from a pattern of whole and half steps: **W W H W W W H**

An easy way to create a major scale is to start with a major pentascale and add 3 notes to the top.

C major scale:

Minor Scales

> A one-octave minor scale is made from a different pattern of whole and half steps: **W H W W H W W**

As you might have guessed, a one-octave minor scale can be built by adding 3 notes to the top of a minor pentascale.

A minor scale:

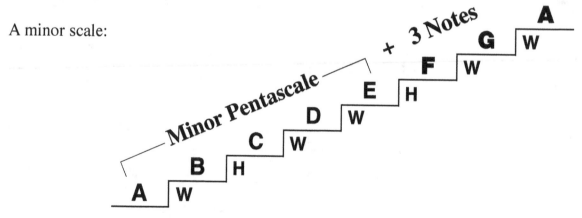

Building Scales from Pentascales

Create major and minor scales by adding 3 notes to the top of these pentascales. Use your keyboard to count the whole and half steps. Remember to include sharps or flats as needed.

C major

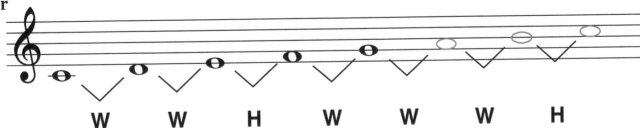

G major

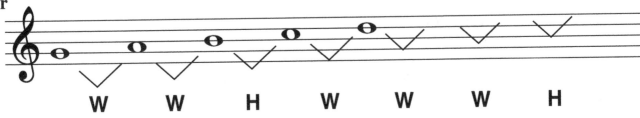

F major

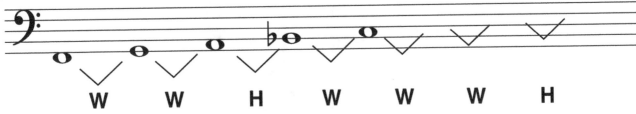

A minor

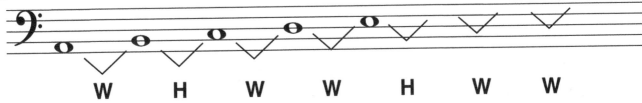

E minor

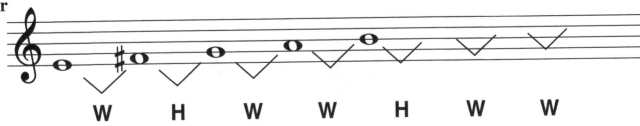

D minor

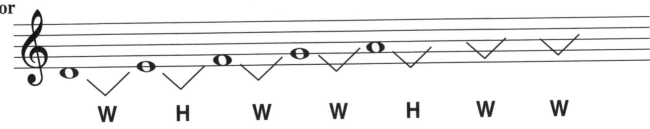

FJH1679

Major and Minor Relatives

Relative major and minor scales have the same sharps or flats in common.

For example:

G major (one sharp - F♯)   E minor (one sharp - F♯)

It's Relatively Simple

To find the *relative minor of any major scale*, **count down 3 half steps** on the keyboard. Notice that you will be **going backward 2 letters** in the musical alphabet.

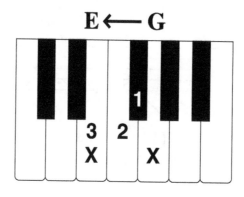

To find the *relative major of any minor scale*, **count up 3 half steps** on the keyboard and **go forward 2 letters** in the musical alphabet.

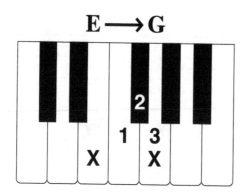

Those Crazy Relatives!

Can you name the relative keys below?
Use your keyboard to count the 3 half steps between relative major and minor.

Review Game

ROCK AROUND THE MUSIC CLOCK!
A journey through all the major and minor keys.

Directions: Visit each of the major and minor keys on the clock below.
As your teacher points to a key, play that major scale and its relative minor.

Note to Teacher: You may request keys in any order, but ask for both the major scale and its relative minor.

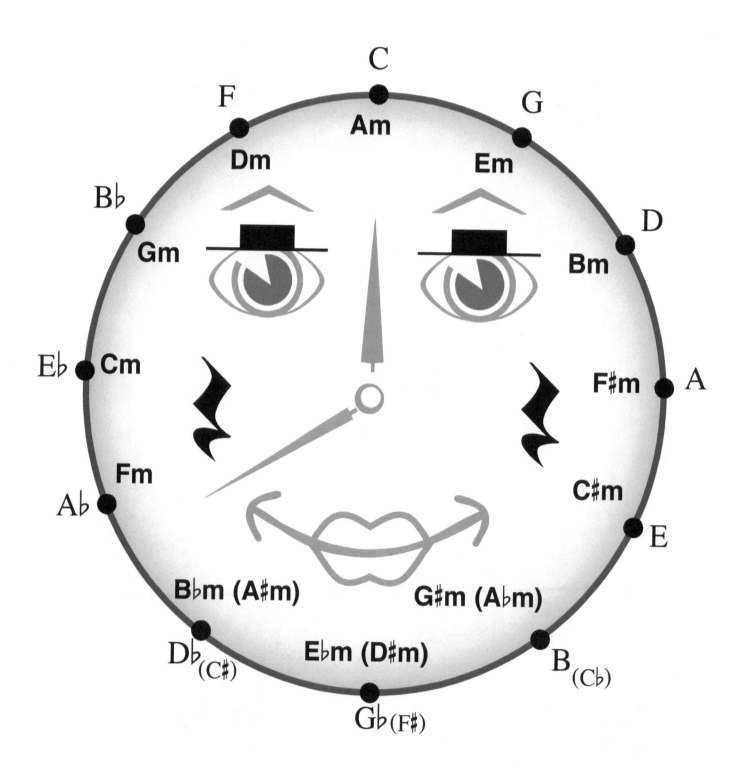

Scale Practice Flashcards

(to add variety to practice)

Student Directions:
Cut out the flashcards by following the dotted lines, and then shuffle them. Draw one from the stack and follow the practice directions on the flashcard. Use scales you have been assigned or other scales of your choice.

CUT HERE

Play *legato* and *forte (f)*.

Play *staccato* and *piano (p)*.

Play your right hand *forte (f)*, and your left hand *piano (p)*.

Play your right hand *piano (p)*, and your left hand *forte (f)*.

Make your scale sound: grumpy, happy, sad (choose one)

(teacher's choice)

Make your scale sound: delicate, strong, jazzy (choose one)

(your choice)